THE

KINGDOM
EMPOWERED
ENTREPRENEUR

THE

KINGDOM
EMPOWERED

ENTREPRENEUR

Awakening Your Supernatural Edge

MATTHEW BELL

Dedication

I dedicate this book to my wife, Kelly. Your creative spirit inspires me. Your unceasing support keeps me going. Love you.

Acknowledgements

First and foremost I would like to thank God for creating me so uniquely and giving me the desire to change the world. Thank You, Jesus!

I'd like to thank my wife Kelly. Without her love and support it would be impossible for me to fulfill my purpose. She has supported me and inspired me daily. Thank you, Kelly!

I'd like to thank my parents for their continued prayers and support. They raised me in the things of God and continue to encourage me today.

To my siblings—Jo, Andy, Sam, and Mary—thanks for being awesome. Y'all the real MVPs.

And to everyone who has mentored me, counseled me, ministered to me, encouraged me, and prayed for me throughout my life, you are far too many to count. I couldn't do it without you. Thank you.

DESTINY IMAGE® PUBLISHERS, INC.

P.O. Box 310, Shippensburg, PA 17257-0310

"Promoting Inspired Lives."

This book and all other Destiny Image and Destiny Image Fiction books are available at Christian bookstores and distributors worldwide.

Cover design by Eileen Rockwell

For more information on foreign distributors, call 717-532-3040.

Reach us on the Internet: www.destinyimage.com.

ISBN 13 TP: 978-0-7684-4896-2

ISBN 13 eBook: 978-0-7684-4897-9

ISBN 13 HC: 978-0-7684-4899-3

ISBN 13 LP: 978-0-7684-4898-6

For Worldwide Distribution, Printed in the U.S.A.

1 2 3 4 5 6 7 8 / 23 22 21 20 19

"You were designed for accomplishment, engineered for success, and endowed with the seeds of greatness."

—Zig Ziglar

Contents

A Note from
the Author

My name is Matthew David Bell. I wake up every morning excited about my day, doing exactly what I love. I am an entrepreneur and I own several businesses. I'm privileged to work with many amazing people on a daily basis. I previously co-founded a mobile app company in 2013, which was acquired by a larger tech company in early 2016. Among other things, I was also a part of the super successful team at a multi-billion dollar tech startup, where I was a key contributor during the company's hyper-growth stage and path toward IPO. I am also a filmmaker, screenwriter, happy husband to a beautiful wife, and a proud dog dad to a nine-pound dachshund.

I am happy to say that today I am living a wonderful and blessed life. However, it took me a while to arrive at the career path that I longed for—to be an entrepreneur.

After college I struggled to understand what I really wanted to do with my life. I tried the corporate world. I even took the LSAT and started the application process to law schools. I've applied to hundreds of different jobs along the way. Nothing felt right unless I was on my own, building stuff, and starting things. I thrive working for myself and I realized in my late twenties that a big part of my purpose in this life is to be an entrepreneur. When I had this revelation it was both liberating, frustrating, exciting, and frightening all at once.

After I realized that God put "entrepreneur" in my DNA when He created me, it took me more than a few years of trying and failing to arrive at success on my own. I had always been successful working for other people's companies, but starting my own companies proved really challenging. I needed to learn practical things I didn't know and spend a ton of time in prayer with God to deal with the emotional ups and downs of starting companies and to remain focused on my dreams and goals for my life.

This book is a personal boot camp for Christian entrepreneurs and folks who are interested in starting a business. It will take you through foundational spiritual and biblical elements that are critical for life as an entrepreneur. There are prayers and exercises at the end of every section to activate the spiritual and practical aspects of what you study each day.

I hope this book blesses you and ignites your entrepreneurial passion! We need more Christian entrepreneurs in the world. Build something.

To your success,
Matthew David Bell

Getting Started

You'll need a notepad or journal for taking notes and completing the exercises at the end of each day. This book is a personal boot camp and a thirty-day journey. I encourage you to dig in, take time, take notes, journal your thoughts, and get creative.

Take your time with the reading each day and then focus on the exercises. This book is designed to impart biblical, spiritual, and practical insights on being an entrepreneur and to ignite your entrepreneurial passion. The exercises are designed to unlock revelation about yourself and draw you closer to God.

Finally, make sure you sign up for my personal newsletter to gain access to special offers, deals, and more!

Go here: www.matthewdavidbell.com/newsletter.

IDENTITY

To understand where God is taking you in business and in life it is important to first know who you are in Christ. Without an understanding of who we are it is difficult for us to achieve that which God has called us to.

These next five days are designed to bring you into a revelation of your identity in Christ.

We love because He first loved us.

1 John 4:19 HCSB

DAY 1

KNOW WHO YOU ARE

The Life-Light was the real thing: every person entering Life he brings into Light. He was in the world, the world was there through him, and yet the world didn't even notice. He came to his own people, but they didn't want him. But whoever did want him, who believed he was who he claimed and would do what he said, he made to be their true selves, their child-of-God selves. These are the God-begotten, not blood-begotten, not flesh-begotten, not sex-begotten.

John 1:9-13 MSG

It is impossible to know what God has called you to do, in business or life in general, without first knowing who you are and who He has created you to be.

You are not what you do, how you look, where you come from, where you've been, your accomplishments, your failures, the job title in front of your name, the PhD after your name, or anything other than this one simple thing: You are a child of God, a son or daughter of the most high King!

God created you in His own image. He calls you son. He calls you daughter. Your value and your worth are intrinsically deposited into your life through God's infinite love for you. Jesus' work on the cross gave your life the value that it has at the very moment you were created. God loved you and knew you before you were even created inside your mother's womb.

God's love for you is so big and so vast that He was willing to send His son to die in your place. Your life was purchased through the sacrifice of another's life—Jesus, God in the flesh. Because of this very fact, your life has a value beyond measure. Your life was purchased with the blood of Christ. Through His Son, God essentially gave His own life for you. That means that the value that God places on your life is on par with Jesus. Why would God sacrifice His only Son to save you, unless the value of your life is truly worth saving?

THE VALUE THAT GOD PLACES ON YOUR LIFE IS ON PAR WITH JESUS.

If it is true that the value of something is
measured by what someone will pay for
it, then we need to rethink our worth.

—Bill Johnson, Sr. Pastor, Bethel Church, Redding, CA

As entrepreneurs, it is important to separate our career identity from our true identity in Christ. We are first a son or daughter of God. Our identity as a child of God is a revelation we need to have before we can operate effectively in any other aspect of our lives, especially business.

Prayer

Father God, give me revelation of the value of my life. Show me what it means to be Your son (or daughter), loved unconditionally and without judgment and without shame. Help me to receive Your love and the revelation of who I am, as Your child, in whom You are well pleased. Amen.

Exercise

✍ Write down three times in your life that you felt truly loved. What were they? Where were you? Who were you with? How did you feel?

✍ Once you have those written down invite the Holy Spirit to be with you and ask God to highlight what He uniquely loves about you. What does the Lord show you?

DAY 2

YOU ARE NOT YOUR MISTAKES

When he was still a long way off, his father
saw him. His heart pounding, he ran out,
embraced him, and kissed him.

Luke 15:20 MSG

You've likely heard the parable of the Prodigal Son, as told by Jesus. The son of a wealthy man demands that his father give him his inheritance at an early age. He runs off and squanders it partying. He ends up destitute with nowhere to go. He decides to return home and plead with his father to allow him to be one of his father's servants, a life that will surely be better than where he has ended up. Yet, his father sees him off in the distance as he is returning and runs to him and embraces his son. The father did not even think about the lost inheritance or the sinfulness of his son's behavior. The father only saw his son. He embraced his son and welcomed him right back into his life through a joyous celebration.

There are two significant details that Jesus intentionally includes in this parable: 1) the father ran to his son, and 2) the father put the family ring on his son's finger. As with all stories in the Bible, it is very important to understand the context of the time that this story was told. In the first century a Middle Eastern man never ran. His garments were too long and he would have to pick them up in order to run without tripping. Doing so would have exposed his bare legs, and it was considered shameful for a man to show his bare legs at this time. Furthermore, the family ring, also known as a signet ring, was much more than a piece of jewelry. The engraving on the ring was used in sealing and authenticating documents for the purposes of conducting business. It was used in conducting financial transactions and business dealings. It would be akin to a father giving his son access to the business checking account today.

THE FATHER ONLY SAW HIS SON, WHOM HE LOVED.

So, what is Jesus actually illustrating through this parable? The son—who squandered his inheritance, sinned against his father and his family, and ended up in a destitute state—was immediately welcomed back into his family by the father. Not only was he welcomed back, but the father was so overjoyed to see his son that he risked public shame and ran to embrace him. And as an even greater display of the father's love and acceptance of his son, he put the family ring on his finger, essentially giving the son full access to the family's wealth.

The father did not see a sinful boy who squandered what was given to him. The father only saw his son, whom he loved.

As you embark upon business ventures of your own, it is very important to leave your mistakes behind you. If you step out to start your own business, it's likely that you will stumble and make mistakes along the way. The entrepreneurial journey is a continual learning experience. Don't let the mistakes you make, or have made in the past, become your identity. Your heavenly Father sees you as His son or daughter, without spot or blemish. He is well pleased with you!

Prayer

Heavenly Father, show me what it means to be Your son (or daughter) whom You fully love, without condition or judgment. Show me what it means to be loved perfectly as Your child no matter what I may have done in the past. You love me because I am Yours. Amen.

Exercise

✍ Write down three times you've made mistakes in life. It can be anything from business to relationships to something you did growing up—anything.

✍ Now, ask God to show you what you learned during the experiences and write down what God shows you.

✍ Spend some time in prayer with God and release any shame, guilt, or regret you may have from these experiences, then ask God to replace the negative feelings with His promises for you.

DAY 3

YOU ARE AN HEIR TO THE KING

Then you will look and be radiant, your heart will throb
and swell with joy; the wealth on the seas will be brought
to you, to you the riches of the nations will come.

Isaiah 60:5 NIV

The promise in God's Word is very clear. Our inheritance is not what we see in the natural, nor what we may be currently experiencing. Our inheritance lies in all that makes up God's Kingdom. If God were to have written a will it would say: "I hereby grant all that is Mine to you." This applies both spiritually and physically. In John 10:10 Jesus said, *"I have come that they may have life, and that they may have it more abundantly."* Our inheritance is for an abundant life and all the goodness of God's Kingdom.

Through our acceptance of Christ we are adopted into God's family as His children. That makes us sons and daughters of the King. That's not just any king. We are children of the almighty God, Maker of heaven and earth—the King of all kings! As God's children we are the rightful heirs to all that is in His Kingdom.

FEAR, WORRY, ANXIETY, DEPRESSION, AND OTHER SUCH THINGS **ARE NOT WHAT GOD HAS GIVEN US AS HIS CHILDREN.**

Spiritually, among other things, the Kingdom of God means peace and joy in the Holy Spirit (see Rom. 14:17). If we are ever experiencing anything outside of peace and joy, then we are not walking in our inheritance. Fear, worry, anxiety, depression, and other such things are not what God has given us as His children. It happens far too often that good, hard-working Christian men and women shy away from opportunities or are too fearful and timid to seize an opportunity that God has laid out before them. In business, and in life, it is important to walk in the revelation that we are heirs to God's Kingdom.

Our inheritance is not only spiritual, but the Lord promises tangible blessings and provisions too! God's Word states that the wealth of sinners is stored up for the godly (see Prov. 13:22). There are opportunities for wealth creation for God's people that have been set aside and stored up for believers in Him. All we have to do is choose to enter into these opportunities and seize that which God has already promised us in His Word.

Now, imagine walking into a boardroom, a sales meeting, or an investor presentation armed with the peace and joy of the Holy Spirit and an expectation that God desires to bless you with the wealth of His Kingdom. That is the revelation God wants us to have. He wants you to flourish and walk in the fullness of the inheritance that He has already laid out before you and promised you in His Word.

Prayer

Heavenly Father, show me what it means to be an heir to Your Kingdom. I desire to walk in the peace and joy of Your Holy Spirit. Fill me with a revelation of my inheritance and show me how to grab hold of it here on earth. Amen.

Exercise

✍ Picture yourself as an heir to a kingdom (because you really are!).

✍ If you had unlimited resources in this life, what are three things that you would create? What would you do? What problems would you solve? What dreams would you pursue?

✍ Think big and write it all down.

DAY 4

YOU HAVE BEEN ADOPTED

For you did not receive the spirit of bondage again to fear, but you received the Spirit of adoption by whom we cry out, "Abba, Father."

Romans 8:15

A very simple summary of biblical history could be described as this: God created man in His image. Man's simple purpose was to tend the garden and have dominion over all of creation. Man sinned and was separated from God through his sin. God, having compassion on man, sent His only Son, Jesus, to die for man's sin and redeem man to the Father.

We have been adopted as sons and daughters of God. And because of God's grace and love, through accepting Jesus Christ's sacrifice, we now have the ability to cry out to God as our "Abba Father." The word *Abba* is an intimate reference to the word *father*. It could be likened to *daddy* or *papa*—an intimate term of endearment that a young child might naturally refer to his father. We are no longer slaves to sin or fear. We have been adopted by God the Father, made possible through the blood of Jesus and His sacrifice on the cross. We have been cleansed from the sin that separated us from the Father and we are no longer called sinners, but we are called sons and daughters of God.

As sons and daughters, adopted by the Father, we have access to the things of heaven, just like a child has access to the things of his earthly father. A child can call his earthly father's name in their home, and his father will respond. A child can run into his earthly father's office and jump on his lap, without appointment, and instantly receive the embrace and love of his father. As sons and daughters of God the Father, we have that same access to God and all of heaven. We can cry out to God, "Abba Father," and the Lord hears all of our cries and prayers.

Why does this matter for life as an entrepreneur or businessperson? It matters greatly! Have you ever felt concern, fear, or anxiety when it comes to matters of business? I certainly have. Doing a big sales pitch or working on a major deal that could impact the outcome of your business can be an all-consuming effort. Fear is often lurking around the corner, waiting to pounce on your weaknesses and cripple you in your ability to be effective. But, as the apostle Paul writes in Romans 8:15, we have not been given a spirit of fear! We have been given a spirit of adoption. We are adopted as sons and daughters of God Almighty, our Father in heaven. Through this spirit of adoption we have unrestricted access to the Father. We can run to Him at any time and cry out "Daddy! I need your help!" and He will always be there to provide love, support, strength, and encouragement, like any loving Father would.

WE CAN RUN TO HIM AT ANY TIME AND CRY OUT "DADDY! I NEED YOUR HELP!" AND HE WILL ALWAYS BE THERE TO PROVIDE LOVE, SUPPORT, STRENGTH, AND ENCOURAGEMENT, LIKE ANY LOVING FATHER WOULD.

Now that you are armed with a greater revelation of your access to God the Father, and knowing that you have been adopted by the Father as His son or daughter, fear has no place in your life.

What will you create now that fear has been removed from your life?

Prayer

Abba Father, thank You for adopting me as Your son (or daughter). Thank You for giving me full access to the things of heaven. I ask that You would take me deeper into my understanding of what it means to be Your son (or daughter). Show me what it means to live a life without fear, as a child of God. Amen.

Exercise

✍ Write a list of ten things that you would pursue if you knew you couldn't fail and had access to unlimited resources to make these things a reality. Briefly explain why you would pursue them. What do these things mean to you? What excites you about them?

✍ What is holding you back from pursuing them now?

DAY 5

YOU HAVE ACCESS TO ALL OF HEAVEN

And God raised us up with Christ and seated us with him in the heavenly realms in Christ Jesus.

Ephesians 2:6 NIV

Now, therefore, you are no longer strangers and foreigners, but fellow citizens with the saints and members of the household of God.

Ephesians 2:19

As a result of Jesus' work on the cross and our acceptance of Jesus as our Lord and Savior, we are no longer slaves to sin. We have been adopted by God the Father as heirs to heaven, and we are now seated in the heavenly realms with Christ Jesus as members of the household of God.

It is important to understand what it truly means to be a member of God's household. The *Merriam-Webster Dictionary* defines *household* as "those who dwell under the same roof and compose a family." God is now our Father and we live with Him as a family in the heavenly realm.

Allow me to offer an analogy. When I was senior in high school I lived with my parents—no surprise there. I would wake up for school, take a shower, get dressed, and run downstairs for breakfast. I'd often grab juice from the refrigerator, cereal from the pantry, and if it was a special day my mom might be making bacon and eggs. As a growing teenager, I'd pretty much eat everything in sight. I'd then hop into my car and drive to school. But, and this may also come as no surprise, I didn't pay for anything! My mom kept the kitchen fully stocked with food, and she paid for all the bathroom products that allowed me to take a morning shower. The clothes I put on were also paid for by my parents. And the car I drove was a gift when I got my license. I had access to all these great things simply by being a member of my father and mother's household. I had full access to the resources of the household.

When I grew up we lived in a modest, middle-class neighborhood, and while we enjoyed comfort we weren't super rich—not by any stretch. While I had access to the wealth and resources of my parents' household, my access was limited to what was available in the household. We didn't have fancy cars, caviar, and designer clothes. But this is where our relationship to God as members of *His* household differs greatly from our experiences with our earthly families. God's household is without limit. All that is good and wonderful and everything you can dream up or desire exists in heaven. Just like how I could walk into my parents' kitchen, open the refrigerator, and pour myself a glass of juice, we can do the same as members of God's household. We simply need to reframe our thinking about what it is that we actually have access to and position ourselves to seek it.

ACCESSING THE THINGS OF HEAVEN IS SOMETHING WE CAN FREELY DO AS THE SONS AND DAUGHTERS OF GOD, AND MEMBERS OF HIS HOUSEHOLD.

Accessing the things of heaven is something we can freely do as the sons and daughters of God, and members of His household. God is not a far-off thing and heaven is not a future reality. Bill Johnson of Bethel Church in Redding, California writes, "The belief that Heaven is entirely a future reality has reduced far too many of God's declarations in Scripture about the believer's identity and calling to 'positional' truths that are acknowledged but never experienced."

Heaven is not a future reality. Heaven is a now reality. We have access to all of heaven today. We simply need to reach for it. When we do, we can see heaven manifest here on earth in all aspects of our lives, including our businesses!

Prayer

Father God, show me what it truly means to be a member of Your household. Show me what it means to have access to all of heaven. I ask that You would make heaven real to my life today and give me the faith to reach for things unseen and usher in breakthrough and heavenly resources into my life today. Amen.

Exercise

✍ Think of one of your life's dreams. Pick one.

_____

_____

_____

_____

_____

_____

_____

✍ Create a list of all the things you would need to turn that dream into a reality.

✍ Now, envision yourself in God's house. Start to prophetically reach out and grab all the things that you need to fulfill this dream.

✍ Declare God's provision over these things and ask Him to physically manifest them in your life so you can pursue your dream.

PURPOSE

You have a unique calling and purpose for your life. Your purpose in life is something only you can fulfill. It is different. It is unique. And God wants to reveal it to you. With revelation of your purpose you will have peace, comfort, and contentment in business and in life.

These next five days are devoted to understanding your purpose in life.

Many are the plans in a person's heart, but it is the Lord's purpose that prevails.

Proverbs 19:21 NIV

DAY 6

YOU HAVE A
UNIQUE PURPOSE

Jesse had seven of his sons pass before Samuel, but Samuel said to him, "The Lord has not chosen these." So he asked Jesse, "Are these all the sons you have?" "There is still the youngest," Jesse answered. "He is tending the sheep." Samuel said, "Send for him; we will not sit down until he arrives." So he sent for him and had him brought in. He was glowing with health and had a fine appearance and handsome features. Then the Lord said, "Rise and anoint him; this is the one."

1 Samuel 16:10-12 NIV

We know that David's purpose in life was not solely to be a shepherd. The Lord's purpose for David was for him to be king. However, it was not known that David would be king until Samuel anointed him in front of his father and brothers when he was a young shepherd boy.

You may not know the fullness of your purpose in life all at once. It may take time for the Lord to fully reveal His path for you and bring you into a place where your purpose is manifested. If you feel trapped or stuck in one place, it is important to trust in what the Lord is doing in your life behind the scenes. Each step you take in business and your entrepreneurial journey is a part of a specific plan as well. Every season of your life has been uniquely designed and is critical in bringing you to the place that God has called you to dwell. These plans help sculpt you into the person God has called you to be. You might not see it clearly as you go through each season, but you will be able to connect the dots as you look back on where you've come from and see what God has taken you through with Him by your side.

DAVID BEGAN HIS LIFE AS A SHEPHERD BOY, **BUT HE ENDED HIS LIFE AS A KING.**

During his Stanford commencement address, Steve Jobs famously said, "You can't connect the dots looking forward; you can only connect them looking backwards. So you have to trust that the dots will somehow connect in your future. You have to trust in something." Steve

Jobs may not have been a Christian, at least not that we are aware of, but we can certainly draw truth from his words. Considering he was one of the most successful and innovative businessmen of all time, he certainly had wisdom and knowledge to impart. As Christians, we know that the "something" we trust in is God.

The Lord is always moving on your behalf. His great love for you continuously calls you into greater intimacy with Him. As you pursue your relationship with God and you are obedient to the process that God is taking you through, you will be able to see the greater purpose God is calling you to through each season and moment in life. The key is to tune in to what the Holy Spirit is speaking to you personally and remain obedient to the assignments the Lord gives you along the way. If you are called to be a future CEO of a Fortune 500 company it is very likely you won't get there overnight. The Lord will take you down many paths and stepping stones before you arrive at a complete picture of your life's purpose. Remember, David began his life as a shepherd boy, but he ended his life as a king.

Prayer

Father God, thank You for the work You are doing in my life. I trust that You have placed a unique purpose on my life. I trust in Your process. I know that Your will and purpose for my life are greater than I could ever imagine. I commit my life's work entirely to You. Amen.

Exercise

✍ Your purpose is often connected to who you are and what you care most deeply about.

✍ Write down ten things you are most passionate about. Explain why you care about each of them.

✍ This exercise will get you thinking about who you really are and what you really love.

DAY 7

THE MOLTING PROCESS

He gives strength to the weary and increases the
power of the weak. Even youths grow tired and
weary, and young men stumble and fall; but those
who hope in the Lord will renew their strength.
They will soar on wings like eagles; they will run and
not grow weary, they will walk and not be faint.

Isaiah 40:29-31 NIV

The eagle is one of God's most majestic creations. Beautiful and graceful, the eagle soars high above the earth, fully free in the purpose the Lord created it to fulfill. The eagle, representing freedom, is even the national symbol of America's identity. The word of the Lord says that those who hope in the Lord will soar like eagles. This is a truly incredible illustration of what we can accomplish, in business and in life, if we simply hope in the Lord.

The use of the eagle imagery by Isaiah is no mistake. The intriguing thing about the eagle is the process it endures at times throughout its life to maintain its God-given purpose. Periodically throughout the eagle's life it must enter into a molting process. During this molting process the mature eagle will partially shed its feathers—its "plumage" as it is referred to. An eagle's plumage can become worn out, and accumulate dirt and oil weighing the eagle down. This wear and tear on its feathers actually makes it harder for the eagle to soar through the sky as God created it to. While not much is known about the specific details of the molting process, many researchers believe it is an essential part of the eagle's journey into maturity. It is believed to be a painful process for the animal, during which the eagle is vulnerable and weakened. While it is uncomfortable, and likely painful for the eagle, the molting process is essential to maintaining its healthy plumage and its ability to soar as the beautiful creature God created it to be.

THERE IS PURPOSE IN ALL THE SEASONS WE GO THROUGH IN LIFE AS ENTREPRENEURS.

You may go through seasons in your life where you may not feel like you are soaring. This can be particularly trying as an entrepreneur when you experience the ups and downs of building your own business. Waiting for a deal to go through, a sale to close, or even losing a valued customer—these things can be challenging! It is all part of the process. Throughout the entrepreneurial journey you will have peaks and valleys, just as we do in every aspect of life. The eagle soars and takes time to renew its strength during the molting process. The Lord says we will soar on wings like eagles if we put our hope in Him.

During the challenging and uncomfortable times, it is critical to put your hope in the Lord. Scripture doesn't say we will be immune to challenges. However, scripture does say that if we hope in the Lord that we will soar like eagles. Just as there is purpose in the molting process for eagles, there is purpose in all the seasons we go through in life as entrepreneurs.

Prayer

Father God, thank You for the promise that I will soar if I put my hope in You. I choose to trust You in all the seasons I go through in business and in life. I choose hope. I will hope in You during the peaks and during the valleys. I will not be deterred. I know that I am called to soar on wings like eagles. I declare my hope is in You. Amen.

Exercise

✍ Write down two to three specific times you felt like you went through a molting process in your life. What did you learn during this experience? How has the experience shaped who you are today? How did you come out stronger and more equipped to "soar" than before you went through it?

_____

_____

_____

_____

_____

_____

_____

_____

_____

_____

_____

_____

DAY 8

YOU ARE CALLED

*God's gifts and God's call are under full
warranty—never canceled, never rescinded.*

Romans 11:29 MSG

Renowned sociologist Robert N. Bellah wrote in his book *Habits of the Heart* that there are three types of people, as it pertains to how humans view their work. The first type of person views his work as a job. This is a typical "nine-to-five" professional. He goes to work, punches a clock, and comes home at the end of the day. The job is essentially a means to paying bills and getting by. The second type of person views his work as a career. This type of person is often much more motivated than the first type of person. He is focused on career advancement and climbing the corporate ladder. The third type of person views his work as his calling. This is where entrepreneurs usually fall. And as Christian entrepreneurs, we know that God is the one who is doing the calling.

I have personally been all three types of these people at one point or another in my life. I have been super motivated about career advancement, only to be beaten down by the process. The pressure to perform and the often underwhelming advancement that came working for other people's companies drove me to become the first type of person—a "nine-to-five" clock puncher. I lost my passion and my work became just a job, going into the office every day, watching the clock, and coming home at five and waking up to do it all over again the next day.

Through climbing the corporate ladder, I realized that I wasn't following my calling. I was following other people. I had developed a belief that "this is what everyone does for success, so I must do it too." After a few years of stumbling my way through the dark in the corporate world I had the profound and liberating revelation of my actual calling. I was called to create and build things of my own. I was called to be an entrepreneur.

YOU ARE NEVER TOO OLD OR TOO OFF TRACK TO FULFILL THE PURPOSE THAT GOD HAS UNIQUELY FASHIONED YOU TO CARRY OUT.

From the moment you choose the path of an entrepreneur you are choosing to follow a very unique calling. Not everyone is cut out for it and not everyone has the DNA for it. It is critically important to be in tune with God's will for your life so you can pursue and execute your calling. It likely will not come to pass overnight. If you take the step to pursue the entrepreneurial path and you commit your pursuit to God, it will come. The fulfillment of your dreams may not happen overnight, but if you surrender your work to the Lord, success will come. God's Word says so.

You are never too old or too off track to fulfill the purpose that God has uniquely fashioned you to carry out. Sam Walton launched the first Wal-Mart in 1962 at the age of 44. Henry Ford created the Model T, the automobile that would revolutionize transportation for the entire world, when he was 45. Ray Kroc launched the McDonald's franchise business at the age of 52, which he grew to the largest fast-food chain in the world. The list of people who found success later on in life goes on and on. It doesn't matter where you are currently in your journey. God has purpose for you, and His timing is never late!

If it seems slow in coming, wait. It's on its way. It will come right on time (Habakkuk 2:3 MSG).

Prayer

Father God, thank You for the promise that the fruit of my calling will come to pass in my life at the right time. I submit my life and my career to Your will. I declare that I am a successful entrepreneur. I am called to carve my own path instead of following the well-traveled road. I declare that the fulfillment of my visions will come to pass. Amen.

Exercise

✍ Write down five times in your life when you felt truly alive and inspired.

_____

_____

_____

_____

_____

✍ What were you doing?

_____

_____

_____

✍ How did these moments feel?

_____

_____

_____

DAY 9

GOD HAS A
HOPE FOR YOU

For I know the thoughts that I think toward you,
says the Lord, thoughts of peace and not of evil,
to give you a future and a hope. Then you will
call upon Me and go and pray to Me, and I will
listen to you. And you will seek Me and find Me,
when you search for Me with all your heart.

Jeremiah 29:11-13

No matter what your current circumstance or situation may be, God has plans for you. His plans include a future and a hope. There is purpose in every day of your life. What you are experiencing today does not indicate what God has laid out before you tomorrow.

What's really interesting about the prophet Jeremiah's words in Jeremiah 29:11-13 is that he was speaking to the Israelites while they were in captivity. The Israelites were in captivity as a result of their disobedience to God. This verse, while a powerful declaration of God's heart for His people, is often taken out of context. To understand the context better, we need to look at Jeremiah 29:7, which reads, *"And work for the peace and prosperity of the city where I sent you into exile. Pray to the Lord for it, for its welfare will determine your welfare"* (NLT).

There are two really interesting things to draw from the context of this passage: 1) God's will in the present doesn't dictate your future; 2) no matter what your circumstance is in the present there is a future and hope in God.

WHERE YOU START IN LIFE DOESN'T DETERMINE WHERE YOU FINISH.

As someone who has personally always identified as an entrepreneur, going back to when I was younger than ten years old, the times that I spent confined to a job and working for other people really did feel like captivity at times! When your vision for your life does not align to your present reality it can be really challenging. All that being said, there is purpose in all the stages of life that God takes you through. Where you start in life doesn't determine where you finish. And despite the challenges of certain seasons, there may be great purpose in the seasons when you feel like you are in a desert or even in your own personal captivity.

I, for one, would not have been equipped to start my own businesses had I not first worked at other companies. I learned practical things like organization, administration, and operations. I also learned spiritual things and acquired spiritual traits such as patience and grace. It's true, while my heart has always longed to have a meaningful impact on the world by creating something of my own, I would not even be equipped to do so had I not first worked for other people. My hope in God was discovered during the process.

Whatever your situation may be today, know that God's heart for your life is full of purpose. You are called to great things. You are destined for greatness. You have the resources of all of heaven available to you. As Jeremiah declared, we must first pray to God and look for Him wholeheartedly. When we do that we will find Him. And in Him we will find revelation of our purpose.

Prayer

Father God, I thank You that Your heart for my life is for me to have a future and a hope. Draw me into You in prayer. Help me to first seek You in all situations. I desire first to seek You. I ask, Lord, that You would give me revelation of my purpose in You. Thank You, Jesus! Amen.

Exercise

✍ Ask God to show you a time (or several times) when you felt like you were in captivity in life. It could be a job you didn't like, a bad relationship experience, or simply a long waiting period as you pursued breakthrough.

✍ Now ask God to show you specifically how He was with you during these times. What is the future and hope that you see for yourself?

DAY 10

YOU ARE ON GOD'S HIGHWAY

A highway shall be there, and a road, and it shall be called the Highway of Holiness. The unclean shall not pass over it, but it shall be for others. Whoever walks the road, although a fool, shall not go astray.

Isaiah 35:8

One of the most common things that Christians struggle with is accurately understanding their purpose in life. A lack of clarity in this area can lead people to a stagnant life, where one spends more time waiting to discover what God has purposed him or her in life, instead of taking action. I have seen countless Christians, earnest in their intentions to do the will of God in their lives, stay put in situations they absolutely despise.

I'd like to offer one example of a young man I met in church years ago. He was a very creative young man, full of ideas, vigor, and passion for the Lord. He was one of those joy-filled folks you see at church with an infectious smile and contagious laughter. Despite his joy in the church environment, he confided in me that he absolutely hated his job. He described it as mundane, boring, and soul-sucking. Yet, when I pressed him about the job and inquired as to why he didn't simply leave to find another job or start a business of his own, something he was truly passionate about, he responded with, "Well, this is my assignment for now, so I'm just going to ask God for the patience to continue to do it."

GOD IS A LOVING FATHER WHO HAS CREATED YOU WITH GREAT PURPOSE.

Dear friends, I'd like to take a moment to clear the air. God is not an abusive Father who has created you to live a life assigned to mundane and boring jobs—far from it! God is a loving Father who has created you with great purpose. What you love, what you care about, your passions and your creativity—these are skills and gifts that God has given you to use while you are in this life. If you don't like your job, you have the power of God and the creativity of the Holy Spirit dwelling inside of you, and you can very easily change your own situation.

This concept may cause concern or confusion at first. If you are like me, you care deeply about doing the will of God in your life and not foolishly following your own ambitions. That's why I have really grabbed hold of Isaiah 35:8 as a foundational principle in my entrepreneurial journey. As an entrepreneur, I have more ideas on a daily basis than I can count. Some are of God and should be pursued. Others are simply creative ideas that will never take form and probably aren't the will of God in my life. But the good news is that, according to Isaiah, not even a fool can go astray! If you are walking with the Lord, though you may have moments of going this way and going that way, you will not go astray. If your heart is truly seeking the Lord, He will continue to draw you toward Himself as you pursue the things in life that He has put in your heart. Your purpose was deposited in you at conception, and God is calling you to step out and pursue it even if you don't yet know what the final outcome looks like.

Prayer

Father God, I trust that You are a loving father and Your will for me is to live a life of joy and fulfillment in You. Help me to trust in my own gifts and skills, the ones You deposited in me at birth, so that I can step out, without fear, and pursue that which You have put on my heart. Amen!

Exercise

✍ Ask the Holy Spirit to highlight three times in your life when you took a wrong turn or made a wrong decision. What were you doing? What was the impact of your choice?

✍ Now ask God to highlight how He turned each one of those situations around and made straight your path. What did God show you throughout the experience? What did you learn throughout the process?

TRUST

When you get on an airplane, you trust that the pilot knows how to fly. If you didn't, I bet you wouldn't get on the plane! The same trust needs to apply to our relationship with God. In life, and in business, it is critical to put our trust fully in the Lord. He is always working on your behalf in everything you do.

These next four days are devoted to strengthening your trust in God.

Trust God from the bottom of your heart;
don't try to figure out everything on your own.
Listen for God's voice in everything you do,
everywhere you go; he's the one who will keep you
on track. Don't assume that you know it all.

Proverbs 3:5 MSG

DAY 11

KEEP YOUR EYES ON JESUS

"Lord, if it's you," Peter replied, "tell me to come to you on the water." "Come," he said. Then Peter got down out of the boat, walked on the water and came toward Jesus. But when he saw the wind, he was afraid and, beginning to sink, cried out, "Lord, save me!" Immediately Jesus reached out his hand and caught him. "You of little faith," he said, "why did you doubt?" And when they climbed into the boat, the wind died down. Then those who were in the boat worshiped him, saying, "Truly you are the Son of God."

Matthew 14:28-33 NIV

As an entrepreneur you are on your own most of the time, especially when starting out. You don't have a boss. You are your own boss. You call the shots and make the big decisions. If there is a fire, you are the one who has to put it out. Depending on what size you grow your company to, and if you hire employees or take on investors, it may remain this way for a while. While on your own it is absolutely critical to your success as an entrepreneur to not rely on yourself but to trust fully in God.

TAKING THE STEP TO START YOUR BUSINESS IS LIKE GETTING OUT OF THE BOAT AND FOLLOWING JESUS TOWARD YOUR CALLING.

Let's use Peter as an example. In the above passage he is in a boat with some of the other disciples and he sees Jesus in the distance walking on the water. Jesus calls to Peter to come to Him and Peter gets out of the boat and starts walking on the water also. This takes guts and faith to do! As Peter is walking on the water the wind picks up and he becomes frightened and cries out for Jesus to save him. Peter became frightened and lost sight of what he was actually doing in the first place—walking on the water!

If God has called you to be an entrepreneur then you ought to take particular note of this story. Taking the step to start your business is like getting out of the boat and following Jesus toward your calling. I guarantee that you will face obstacles and challenges of all sorts along the way.

If you lose sight of the fact that God has called you to do this, you too will become frightened. As an entrepreneur it is critically important to stay focused on where you are going, not what you are going through. If Peter had stayed focused on Jesus and not on the storm around him, he would have been able to continue toward his end goal without fear or concern. Sure, the wind and the waves were probably scary looking, but only if they are your focus instead of Jesus.

AS AN ENTREPRENEUR IT IS CRITICALLY IMPORTANT TO STAY FOCUSED ON WHERE YOU ARE GOING, NOT WHAT YOU ARE GOING THROUGH.

Obstacles and challenges will come and go every day in your life as an entrepreneur. Jesus will never change. He is the same yesterday, today, and forever.

> *Keep your eyes on Jesus, who both began and finished this race we're in. Study how he did it. Because he never lost sight of where he was headed* (Hebrews 12:2 MSG).

Prayer

*Father God, help me to look to You at all times
in my business and my daily walk with You.
Give me the strength to persevere during storms
and not be distracted with what's going on in
my circumstances. I choose to put my faith in
You and keep my eyes fixed on Jesus. I trust that
You will help me every step of the way. Amen.*

Exercise

✍ Think of three times in life when you had to do something new, scary, or risky. What were they? How did you feel before taking the leap? How was God involved in the process? How did God help you as you were stepping out?

_____

_____

_____

_____

✍ Ask the Holy Spirit to show you how God was supporting you in ways you may not have been aware of at the time. Write down what God shows you.

_____

_____

_____

_____

DAY 12

TRUST THROUGH OBEDIENCE

If you listen obediently to the Voice of God, your God, and heartily obey all his commandments that I command you today, God, your God, will place you on high, high above all the nations of the world. All these blessings will come down on you and spread out beyond you because you have responded to the Voice of God, your God: God's blessing inside the city, God's blessing in the country; God's blessing on your children, the crops of your land, the young of your livestock, the calves of your herds, the lambs of your flocks. God's blessing on your basket and bread bowl; God's blessing in your coming in, God's blessing in your going out. God will defeat your enemies who attack you. They'll come at you on one road and run away on seven roads. God will order a blessing on your barns and workplaces; he'll bless you in the land that God, your God, is giving you.

Deuteronomy 28:1-8 MSG

Entrepreneurs move at light speed. There is more to do each day than can possibly be accomplished. Entrepreneurs have to make split-second decisions and act decisively all day long, day in and day out. It is nearly impossible to act according to God's will for your business if you are not in tune to the Holy Spirit and God's voice in your life.

WE MUST INVITE THE HOLY SPIRIT TO DWELL IN OUR BUSINESSES WITH US SO THAT WE REMAIN CONTINUOUSLY IN TUNE WITH GOD'S VOICE THROUGHOUT THE DAY.

As an entrepreneur, it is important to be intentional about taking time to listen to God all throughout your day. This doesn't mean that you have to stop what you are doing every time you need to make a decision. For instance, it wouldn't be realistic to put a sales call on hold to go spend time in prayer to figure out what to say next while you're in the middle of making your pitch. That's not the point! The point is that we must invite the Holy Spirit to dwell in our businesses with us so that we remain continuously in tune with God's voice throughout the day. When we do this, even those split-second decisions will be supernaturally influenced by the voice of God and our decisions will move us forward in the will of God.

I try to take moments throughout the day to find a quiet conference room in my office building (or even the stall in the restroom!) to collect myself, refresh spiritually, and invite God's presence to fill the atmosphere. Every time I do this I emerge energized and ready to take on whatever is up next, with the Holy Spirit guiding my every action and decision. It is important to take time to rest throughout the day and invite God to take the lead.

The above referenced passage from Deuteronomy plainly states if you listen obediently to God, He will bless you. Period! It really is a simple formula. If you don't already do so, I suggest you start your workday with prayer. Invite the Holy Spirit to walk with you all throughout your day. Periodically take moments to spend time with God, even if it is just a minute. When you invite God to be with you throughout the day, it is easier to hear His voice and be obedient to how He is guiding your actions.

Prayer

Holy Spirit, I invite Your presence to be with me wherever I go and in whatever I do. I want to hear the voice of my heavenly Father guiding my every decision. Help me to be in tune and obedient to Your Spirit in my work and life. Remind me to take time throughout my day to refresh in Your presence. Amen.

Exercise

✍ Take a moment and invite the Holy Spirit to be with you. Wait on God and recognize His presence when the Holy Spirit manifests Himself. Stay in this place for a few minutes then ask God to show you a vision for where He wants you to go next. What is the first next step He is directing you to take? What does this look like? Write down what you see.

_____

_____

_____

_____

✍ Start your day like this tomorrow morning too. Then at the end of the day write down how your day went. Was it different from other days? Were you in tune with God's guidance throughout your day? How so?

_____

_____

_____

_____

DAY 13

COMMIT YOUR BUSINESS TO GOD

We can make our own plans, but the Lord gives the right answer. People may be pure in their own eyes, but the Lord examines their motives. Commit your actions to the Lord, and your plans will succeed.

Proverbs 16:1-3 NLT

The scripture above is both a promise and a command. God promises that our plans will succeed. However, there is a condition. In order for our plans to succeed we must first put God in charge of our work. The translation from the Amplified Bible provides even more substance and clarity on the condition: *"Commit your works to the Lord [submit and trust them to Him], and your plans will succeed [if you respond to His will and guidance]."* Your plans will succeed *if* you commit your works to God and you respond to God's will and guidance.

NO MATTER WHAT WE DO, IF WE WANT IT TO SUCCEED, WE NEED TO PUT THE LORD FIRST.

The Bible says that we will be successful if we trust the Lord with our work and respond to His will and guidance. That seems simple enough, but how simple is it really? How many of us actually take the time daily, or ever, to outwardly commit our work to the Lord? The Holy Spirit had to give me revelation of how important it is to do this, before I really began practicing it myself. Committing our work to God is critical for entrepreneurs, as well as all followers of Christ. No matter what we do, if we want it to succeed, we need to put the Lord first.

Here are three practical steps that you can take to always put God in charge of your work:

1. At the onset of every new business or project take the time to say a prayer like this: "Lord, I put You in charge of [insert name of business or project]; I declare You as the leader of my work and I submit to Your will. Guide me in all that I do." Feel free to adapt this to your own words, of course. Just make sure to dedicate your work to the Lord in the very beginning, as the Bible encourages us to.

2. Start every day with a prayer, dedicating your day and all the work and decisions of that day to the Lord. Here is one that I like to say in the mornings: "I lift my hands to the most high God and declare His rule in my life and all that pertains to me!" Raise your hands and belt it out. I don't remember to do it every day, but it makes a very powerful difference when I do remember to start my day with it.

3. Pray about all big decisions. When faced with a decision in business, I don't make the decision without first seeking the Lord's guidance and asking the Holy Spirit to speak to me about what I should do. When under time constraints and pressure from work, it is critical to pause and seek God. You may not feel fully confident in the path you should go, but as long as you make your decision by seeking God, the Lord will guide you.

Prayer

Father God, I choose to trust in You as the master of my work. I put You in charge of all that I do. I ask that Your Spirit would remind me daily to submit my work and decisions to You. Remind me to pause and seek You in all decisions and matters of life and business. Amen.

Exercise

✍ Think of three things that are currently on your mind. They can be business or personal, whatever you want. Write them down and submit them to God.

_____

_____

_____

✍ Ask the Holy Spirit to show you three negative thoughts that have caused you to worry or stress. Write them down.

_____

_____

_____

✍ Now ask God to give you three promises to replace the negative ones. Declare these promises over your life. What does God show you through this process? Write it down.

_____

_____

_____

DAY 14

FAITH COMES FROM HEARING

*So then faith comes by hearing, and
hearing by the word of God.*

Romans 10:17

Trust and faith go hand in hand. The very act of trusting God is putting your faith in Him and not yourself. You may not know the outcome. The circumstance before you may look bleak. You may have a thousand reasons to doubt that your situation will turn out for your good and God's glory. But none of that matters when you have faith in God. For it is when you put your faith completely in Him that you are able to trust in His outcome. Our focus should be on building our faith through the Word of God, for as our faith grows, so does our ability to trust.

AS OUR FAITH GROWS, SO DOES OUR ABILITY TO TRUST.

As scripture puts it, faith comes by hearing the Word of God. The more of the Word of God you hear, the greater your faith builds within you. There is something different about hearing spoken words, both God's Word and the words of man, that has a stronger impact on us than merely reading or seeing words. By way of example, a child growing up with a critical mother or father who always hears words of criticism may develop a low self-esteem and could grow up doubting himself. Conversely, if a child grows up with very supportive parents, who are continually supporting him with their words and encouraging him, he could grow up with great confidence and a fearless pursuit of his dreams. Words really matter, especially spoken words.

Despite your upbringing or the influence of your father and mother, we all now have the opportunity to develop a mindset of supernatural faith that is rooted in trusting God. We can rewire our entire thinking by washing our minds in the Word of God. There are two obvious ways to achieve this: 1) Go to a good Bible-based church that preaches the Word of God, and 2) read the Word aloud to yourself as you study it on your own. If the second one sounds silly, I assure you it is not! It is a simple and effective way to let the Word of God flow through you and back into your own ears so that you may hear the Word magnified by your own voice and illuminated by the Holy Spirit. Something supernatural occurs when we do this.

OUR WALK WITH THE LORD IS A JOURNEY OF TRANSFORMATION.

When we shift our focus to hearing God's voice through the Word and not the voice of man or the voice of the enemy, we are able to supernaturally reframe our thinking to align with what God thinks about us and to continually transform our minds to truth. When we are born again we are not immediately perfect—far from it! Scripture plainly states, in Second Corinthians 3:18, *"But we all, with unveiled face, beholding as in a mirror the glory of the Lord, are **being transformed** into the same image from glory to glory, just as by the Spirit of the Lord."* Our walk with the Lord is a journey of transformation. It is a process, not a fully completed act at the moment of salvation. Yes, salvation is an instantaneous and miraculous event that occurs when we accept Jesus as our Lord and Savior, but that is also the beginning of the process of transformation.

It is when faith rises up within us that we are enabled to put our trust fully in God's hands for all aspects of life from business to relationships to family and everything else. It is by hearing the word that our faith supernaturally grows.

Prayer

Father God, I ask that You would grow in me a faith like never before. I desire the faith that allows me to put my trust fully in You, God. As I hear the Word of God, I ask that You would accelerate the growth of faith in me. By faith, I put my trust in You. Amen.

Exercise

✍ Write down three Bible verses that are particularly meaningful for your life right now. Use Google if you need to. Then spend five minutes reading them out loud and speaking them over your life. How do you feel after? Write it down.

_____

_____

_____

_____

_____

_____

_____

✍ Make this a practice throughout your day. If the day gets stressful, speak the Word out loud over your situation. Keep the three Bible verses you wrote down in your pocket and pull them out as needed throughout your day. Do this for a few days this week and write down how you feel. Do you notice a difference?

GIFTS

God created each person uniquely.
The Lord gave each of us a different set
of gifts and talents. It is important to
understand your unique set of gifts so
you can effectively put them to use in
fulfilling the calling of God on your life.

These next four days are devoted to
understanding your own unique gifts.

---

*Since we have gifts that differ according
to the grace given to us, each of us
is to use them accordingly.*

Romans 12:6 AMP

DAY 15

YOU ARE UNIQUELY GIFTED

God has given each of you a gift from his great variety of spiritual gifts. Use them well to serve one another.

1 Peter 4:10 NLT

What God has called you to do in life only you are uniquely gifted to carry out. You have all that you need spiritually to be all that God has called you to be. The moment you were knitted inside your mother's womb, the Lord created you with all that you will need to fulfill your life's purpose. The moment you accepted Christ as your Lord and Savior the Holy Spirit made His home in your heart, making possible the manifestation of that which God has called you to fulfill in your life.

If you haven't noticed already, everyone is different. The people around you will find success differently and in different timelines than you. It is important that we never compare ourselves to someone else's success or journey. That would be a fruitless waste of energy. Everyone is called to do something different and your purpose is something that only you can fulfill. No one else can do it! To fulfill your God-given purpose and calling, you will need to use the unique set of gifts that God has given to you. This is particularly important to understand as you set out on your entrepreneurial journey.

When God sent the angel Gabriel to Nazareth to announce to the young Virgin Mary that she was highly favored by the Lord and she would soon bear a child, Mary was confused and "greatly troubled," it says in the Bible. After all, it's not every day you are told you are going to give birth to the savior of the world as a virgin!

IF THE LORD HAS CALLED YOU TO IT, YOU HAVE ALL THAT YOU NEED AND ARE READY FOR THE TASK!

But the angel said to her, "Do not be afraid, Mary; you have found favor with God. You will conceive and give birth to a son, and you are to call him Jesus. He will be great and will be called the Son of the Most High. The Lord God will give him the throne of his father David, and he will reign over Jacob's descendants forever; his kingdom will never end." "How will this be," Mary asked the angel, "since I am a virgin?" (Luke 1:30-34 NIV)

The angel Gabriel then explains to Mary that the Holy Spirit will come upon her, and the power of the Most High will overshadow her, and "no word from God will ever fail." Despite what the word from God may sound like, or how impossible it looks, it is so important to have revelation of the truth that God's word never fails. If God speaks that a virgin will conceive a child, it will be done, regardless of how physically impossible that may look in the natural.

Just as the Lord spoke to Mary and set her aside to be the mother of Jesus, if the Lord has spoken to your heart to start a business of your own, don't be concerned when you face challenges or obstacles or if something looks impossible. If the Lord has called you to it, you have all that you need and are ready for the task!

Prayer

*Father God, I ask that You would give me
revelation of my unique gifts and skills
that You have given me, and only me.
Help me to understand how to use what
You have given me to carry out my unique
purpose and calling in life. Amen.*

Exercise

✍ List five things that you are really good at and better at than most other people. (It's okay to be confident in your God-given gifts and skills!)

✍ Ask God to show you at least one specific moment you used each of these gifts successfully. These can be work or personal examples.

✍ Now spend some time in prayer and ask God to increase these gifts in your life and open opportunities to use them even more.

DAY 16

EVERYONE IS GIFTED DIFFERENTLY

For just as each of us has one body with many members, and these members do not all have the same function, so in Christ we, though many, form one body, and each member belongs to all the others. We have different gifts, according to the grace given to each of us. If your gift is prophesying, then prophesy in accordance with your faith; if it is serving, then serve; if it is teaching, then teach; if it is to encourage, then give encouragement; if it is giving, then give generously; if it is to lead, do it diligently; if it is to show mercy, do it cheerfully.

Romans 12:4-8 NIV

Your calling is different. Your path in life is exclusively yours. The gifts that God has given you are suited to fulfill your specific calling in life, not someone else's. When uniquely and diversely gifted people come together as one body, our gifts complement each other's. If everyone had the same set of gifts, then the world would suffer greatly from boredom. Just as the human body needs arms, legs, fingers, and toes to serve different functions for the body, churches operate best when each uniquely gifted human operates where he or she is best skilled. This is the same for companies and businesses.

Let's take a look at a real-world example of how two different gifts work together for the good of a business—software engineers and salespeople.

If you are in the technology industry, you likely have a team of engineers building and working hard on your product. They are meticulous, detail-oriented, and super focused on their unique work. It is highly differentiated and technical work. Most of us don't know how to do it, nor would we have the temperament to do it if we tried. They build the products we use every day—Facebook, Instagram, Twitter—you name it and engineers were the ones who built it. They often work plugged into headphones, not looking up from their code for hours at a time.

CHURCHES OPERATE BEST
WHEN EACH UNIQUELY
GIFTED HUMAN OPERATES
WHERE HE OR SHE IS BEST
SKILLED.

Once products are built, they don't make money on their own. The businesspeople of the tech company are the ones who make it possible for the elegant product that the engineers built to make money for the business. As of writing this, Facebook has a market cap of $400 billion. That is due in large part to the incredible advertising engine that Facebook's engineers created. That advertising engine makes money because of the salespeople who sell the ads that generate the company's revenue. Facebook's ads are what earn shareholders lots of money and keep the lights on at Facebook's headquarters.

Engineers have their gifts. Salespeople and business folks have their gifts too. They are very different gifts and skill sets, but together they produce significantly more value than would be achievable separately. In business it is critically important to know which gifts you possess and which you do not possess. This will allow you to stay focused on areas where you can personally produce the best fruit and will give you an understanding of the types of people you need to surround yourself with to complement your own unique gifts.

Prayer

Father God, I thank You for my unique gifts. I ask that You would help me to see how my gifts work alongside other people's gifts. I ask that You would bring the right business partners, employees, and colleagues into my life so that we can strengthen each other through our complementary gifts and skills. Amen.

Exercise

✍ List three times you partnered with someone who had a different set of skills than you did. It could be a project, business, mission trip, or anything else.

_____

_____

_____

✍ What did you bring to the table? What did he or she bring to the table? How did your unique skills complement each other? Write it all down.

_____

_____

_____

DAY 17

YOUR GIFTS WILL BRING YOU PEACE AND JOY

Before I formed you in the womb I knew
you, before you were born I set you apart; I
appointed you as a prophet to the nations.

Jeremiah 1:5 NIV

Just as the Lord spoke to Jeremiah in the passage above, He has done the same for you. You may not have heard the audible voice of God in regard to His will and calling for your life, but the truth is that before the Lord created you, and even before He created the world, He thought of you. He thought of what gifts He would give you. He thought of what He would use you to accomplish in your life and your time in the world. We may not receive a step-by-step plan that shows us exactly what to do and how to do it. However, the gifts the Lord has given us are easy for us to see at work in our lives. When we operate in our God-given gifts it releases joy and peace in our lives. We may not have the full picture of our purpose and calling, but with an understanding of our gifts we have a good starting place.

JUST AS A BIRD IS AT HOME FLYING THROUGH THE SKY, AND A FISH CAN GRACEFULLY SWIM THROUGH THE OCEAN, WHEN WE USE OUR GOD-GIVEN GIFTS WE ARE OPERATING IN THE ENVIRONMENT GOD HAS GIFTED US FOR OUR SUCCESS.

So, what are you gifted to do? That should be a somewhat straightforward question to answer. Your God-given gifts are the things you can do naturally well, with very little or no training. We are all capable of learning anything we set our minds to. But what are the things you are really good at without trying? It may be public speaking, writing, math, or building things. When you focus on doing the things you are good at, you are exercising the gifts that the Lord, your Creator, has given you. It is in doing what God has gifted us to do that we are able to have joy and peace. It is not hard. It doesn't require striving. Just as a bird is at home flying through the sky, and a fish can gracefully swim through the ocean, when we use our God-given gifts we are operating in the environment God has gifted us for our success.

What would happen if you tried to make a fish fly? You could take a fish out of its natural habitat and throw it into the air, but would that do any good? Or what would happen if you tried to make a bird live under the water? I suspect that the results of either attempt would not be too positive for the animal! The same is true for humans. If we operate where we are gifted, it brings peace and joy. We feel at home operating in our gifts. If we try to copy others or follow someone else's gifts, that may not result in peace or joy. Copying someone else could lead to stress, fear, anxiety, and a feeling of striving toward a goal that may or may not ever arrive.

I'm not suggesting we can't learn new skills and talents. We can do all things through Christ who gives us strength! (See Philippians 4:13.) However, if we start by focusing on where God has already gifted us we will operate in a place of peace and joy. Then the rest will come much more easily. As you embark on your entrepreneurial journey, I highly recommend starting in an area you already know well and feel comfortable. Let your God-given gifts guide you, and the Holy Spirit will show you the path.

Prayer

Father God, I ask that You would illuminate where You have uniquely gifted me. Show me the gifts, skills, and talents that You have given me. I desire to use these gifts so that I can be effective in my own life and minister to others both spiritually and professionally by honoring You. Amen.

Exercise

✍ Write down five things you love to do and five things you really don't like to do. What you enjoy in life is often an indication of how you are gifted. What you don't like to do may be an indication of a weakness or an area for improvement (we all have areas where we can improve!).

_____

_____

_____

_____

_____

_____

_____

_____

_____

✍ Ask God to show you how to open up opportunities to do more of that which you love to do and for Him to give you practical steps to help you convert your weaknesses into strengths. Write down what God reveals to you.

DAY 18

USE YOUR GIFTS

For to everyone who has, more will be given, and he will have abundance; but from him who does not have, even what he has will be taken away.

Matthew 25:29

In the Parable of the Talents, found in Matthew 25:14-30, Jesus tells the story of a master embarking on a journey who entrusts his three servants with different portions of talents to steward in his absence. One he gives five, another he gives two, and another he gives one. The servants who were given five and two talents each went out and traded wisely with what their master had given them, ultimately doubling their portion. The servant who was given one talent fearfully buried the talent and did nothing with it. In his foolish logic, he assumed it would be safer for him and his master to simply bury and preserve what he had been given. Upon the master's return, the two servants who doubled their portions were rewarded by the master. The servant who hid his one talent was scorned by his master for having acted foolishly and fearfully, and the master cast him out of his presence.

This parable lays ground for a very powerful message, particularly when it comes to life as an entrepreneur or for anyone who desires to live out his or her God-given purpose. It is very simply this: God wants you to use your gifts! God has gifted each of His creations with a unique set of gifts. Our gifts are tools that God has fashioned for us to use in the pursuit of our purpose. Not using your gifts due to fear, worry, insecurity, or simply because you feel comfortable where you are is exactly what the enemy wants. It may be that the area where God has gifted you is an area you feel insecurity, fear, or doubt. That is very likely the enemy's tactic to divert you away from focusing on something that God has actually gifted you to succeed in!

Let me offer an example from my own life. When I was younger I was terrified of public speaking. I used to freeze up, forget my words, and stumble over myself. As I grew up and I matured in Christ I felt that I had a preaching gift and was called to speak publicly. This was confirmed by leaders in my life and many prophetic words declared over me before I had ever preached a word publicly. God opened up the doors for me to have a regular preaching position at an inner-city mission church and I was both excited and terrified. I was excited to use this gift that I believed God had given me, but I was terrified because my only experiences with public speaking up until that point had been epic failures. This time was different. I felt the anointing of God on this opportunity and I was determined to walk out my calling and use my God-given gifts!

> # GOD WANTS YOU TO USE YOUR GIFTS! OUR GIFTS ARE TOOLS THAT GOD HAS FASHIONED FOR US TO USE IN THE PURSUIT OF OUR PURPOSE.

I remember the first day I was scheduled for preaching. I was nervous, but committed. I had such nerves walking into the church that I was sweating. But something happened that day as I stepped out in faith to use my gifts. I believe that God honored my obedience to the call He had put on my life and gave me the grace I needed to overcome my fear and preach the Word of God with conviction and power. As I grabbed hold of the microphone to preach publicly for the first time, fear was replaced by courage, and the anointing of the Holy Spirit came into the building. People were saved, healed, and delivered, and that was the beginning of my public preaching ministry. I never again had fear, worry, or doubt about public speaking. I grew in confidence in my speaking abilities, and the Lord used me in many situations to bring the lost to salvation.

The Lord wants you to use your gifts in your business and ministry. Don't bury them or set them aside for a later time. Ask God for the grace and courage to step out and put your gifts to use. He gave them to you to use, not to hide away.

Prayer

Father God, thank You for my unique gifts that You have given me. I want to use them to the fullest in this life! I ask that You would reveal to me all the areas where You have gifted me, and I ask that You would give me the grace and courage to step out of my comfort zone to put my gifts to use for Your glory, as I pursue the purpose You have for my life. Amen!

Exercise

✍ Sometimes the enemy will try to make us feel weak or insecure in certain areas, like my personal example with public speaking. But God is way bigger!

✍ Write down five things you love to do and five things you really don't like to do. What you enjoy in life is often an indication of how you are gifted. What you don't like to do may be an indication of a weakness or an area for improvement (we all have areas where we can improve!).

_____

_____

_____

_____

✍ Ask God to show you how to open up opportunities to do more of that which you love to do and for practical steps to help you convert your weaknesses into strengths. Write down what God reveals to you.

OVERCOMING

When Jesus died on the cross and rose again
He defeated death, and the war was won.
Even though the war is already won, battles
will still remain in this life. With Jesus,
we have all that we need to conquer and
overcome all spiritual and physical obstacles
that come against us and our businesses.

These next four days are devoted to
empowering you to conquer obstacles in life.

---

*For we are not fighting against flesh-and-
blood enemies, but against evil rulers and
authorities of the unseen world, against
mighty powers in this dark world, and
against evil spirits in the heavenly places.*

Ephesians 6:12 NLT

DAY 19

DEALING WITH
THREATS HEAD-ON

*Benaiah son of Jehoiada, a valiant fighter from
Kabzeel, performed great exploits. He struck down
Moab's two mightiest warriors. He also went down
into a pit on a snowy day and killed a lion.*

1 Chronicles 11:22 NIV

Benaiah is an interesting character in the Bible. He is described as one of David's mighty warriors, having performed great exploits. The really interesting thing mentioned about Benaiah in Scripture is when he slew a lion in a pit on a snowy day. This is not a commonly told Bible story, but there is so much we can gain from it that it should be!

IF YOU BECOME AWARE OF SOMETHING NEAR TO YOUR BUSINESS THAT COULD POTENTIALLY POSE A RISK, WOULD YOU JUST LET IT BE OR WOULD YOU ADDRESS IT?

Through Scripture we know that the lion often represents the enemy. *"Be alert and of sober mind. Your enemy the devil prowls around like a roaring lion looking for someone to devour"* (1 Pet. 5:8 NIV). But what threat does a lion in a pit pose to us? It's stuck down in the pit, out of the way, and causing no harm. So, why did Benaiah take the risk to go down into the pit to kill the lion?

The lion, whether contained in a pit or roaming around nearby, is your enemy. Think of the lion in terms of risks and threats to your business. If you become aware of something near to your business that could potentially pose a risk, would you just let it be or would you address it?

Even if the risk appears contained for the moment, what if it escalated and became a very present threat to the health of your business? If the lion got loose from the pit, then surely he would have presented a very real threat to Benaiah. His life would have been in danger! The most interesting thing about Benaiah's character is that he didn't wait until the lion endangered him. He identified something that could be a threat to his life and went out of his way to kill it.

As entrepreneurs and businesspeople we will continually encounter risks and threats to our businesses, big and small, obvious and elusive, internal and external. Sometimes risks are very clear and present; other times the most lethal threats to our business will elude us until they manifest with devastating results. If we identify a potential risk, it may prove critical to address the risk head-on, just like Benaiah eliminated the lion.

As Christians in the business world, we have a distinct advantage over our competition—the power of God! Through prayer and our relationship with the Holy Spirit, we gain supernatural insight into anything that may rise up against our businesses and us personally. All we need to do is put our trust in the Lord and listen to His voice, and He will protect us in all that we do.

AS CHRISTIANS IN THE BUSINESS WORLD, **WE HAVE A DISTINCT ADVANTAGE OVER OUR COMPETITION— THE POWER OF GOD!**

So do not fear, for I am with you; do not be dismayed, for I am your God. I will strengthen you and help you; I will uphold you with my righteous right hand (Isaiah 41:10 NIV).

Prayer

Lord, I choose to hide myself in You and give to You all that I do in my life. Make all risks to my business known, and give me supernatural insights in how to deal with them head-on. I ask that You would protect my business from harm so we both may flourish. Amen.

Exercise

✍ Ask God to highlight five things that could pose a risk to your business. If you don't currently have a business then pick one of your business ideas. Write down what God shows you.

_____

_____

_____

_____

_____

✍ Now ask God to prophetically give you guidance for how you should handle these risks before they manifest into a real threat.

DAY 20

COUNT IT JOY

*Consider it a sheer gift, friends, when tests and
challenges come at you from all sides. You know that
under pressure, your faith-life is forced into the open
and shows its true colors. So don't try to get out of
anything prematurely. Let it do its work so you become
mature and well-developed, not deficient in any way.*

James 1:2-4 MSG

In business, and in life, you are going to face challenges and obstacles. The Bible never says that once you become a Christian life becomes easy and free of all difficulty. It's quite the opposite. Once you become a Christian the enemy now wants to take you out! The light in you is a threat to the darkness. What the Bible does say is to *consider it a gift when tests and challenges come at you from all sides.*

Why would God want us to view tests and challenges as a gift? They are hard and no fun! There's a well-known quote that says, "If God brought you to it, He'll bring you through it." God doesn't give us any easy path in life just because we choose to follow Him. He gives us the strength we need to take on any challenge that comes at us.

By way of example, let's look at the life of King David. Just like us, God's calling for David's life was placed on him before he was born. God had chosen David to be king of Israel from the moment he was conceived and knit within his mother's womb. Despite the powerful destiny that God had laid out before him, David still had to overcome many challenges and obstacles before arriving at his position as king over Israel. He fought lions and bears in the wilderness, ran from his predecessor Saul who wanted him dead, and had to take on a giant all by himself. These are just a few of the challenges that David faced along the way to his position as king.

When David was still a shepherd boy the Philistine army gathered their forces and prepared to attack the Israelites. One Philistine in particular, the giant Goliath, taunted and tormented the Israelites, all of whom were too timid and fearful to confront Goliath one on one. But David was not afraid. He told Saul himself that he would take on Goliath and fight him. What follows is one of the most notable and retold stories in the history of the world. David, a young boy, defeated the enemy's war-rior giant with nothing more than a sling and five smooth stones.

GOD DOESN'T GIVE US ANY EASY PATH IN LIFE JUST BECAUSE WE CHOOSE TO FOLLOW HIM. HE GIVES US THE STRENGTH WE NEED TO TAKE ON ANY CHALLENGE THAT COMES AT US.

David said to the Philistine, "You come against me with sword and spear and javelin, but I come against you in the name of the Lord Almighty, the God of the armies of Israel, whom you have defied. This day the Lord will deliver you into my hands, and I'll strike you down and cut off your head. This very day I will give the carcasses of the Philistine army to the birds and the wild animals, and the whole world will know that there is a God in Israel. All those gathered here will know that it is not by sword or spear that the Lord saves; for the battle is the Lord's, and he will give all of you into our hands" (1 Samuel 17:45-47 NIV).

When facing challenges and obstacles in your business it is important to remember two things: 1) Count it as a gift, because the experience will transform you; 2) the battle is the Lord's!

Prayer

*Father God, remind me to look to You when
I face challenges and obstacles in my life
and in my business. Your Word says that
I will become mature and well developed
during the process. I give my battles to You
so that you may fight them for me. Amen.*

Exercise

✍ Take a moment and write down three times you faced a giant in your life and won. It could be anything from confronting someone, a major test in school, a big sales pitch, or even riding a bike for the first time.

_____

_____

_____

✍ What did you learn during each experience? How did God use these experiences to develop you and mature you? Write down what God reveals to you.

_____

_____

_____

DAY 21

PERMISSION
TO FAIL

Have I not commanded you? Be strong and courageous!
Do not be terrified or dismayed (intimidated), for
the Lord your God is with you wherever you go.

Joshua 1:9 AMP

"Failure is a detour, not a dead-end street," according to the Christian businessman and motivational speaker, Zig Ziglar. Failure should really be viewed as a stepping-stone to success. It should not be viewed as an obstacle preventing you from achieving your goals. In business, and in life, it is critical to break away from the fear of failure so you can discover a life of unbridled freedom. Everyone fails along the way. It is how we move forward after a failure that determines the outcome in our lives.

At some point or another it happens to everyone who tries to do something new, whatever that "something" may actually be. Even the most successful people in the history of the world have failed somewhere along the way. Thomas Edison, Steve Jobs, Henry Ford, Bill Gates, and Walt Disney, among many other very notably successful people, all failed before becoming the successes that we remember them as today.

Failure is part of life. No one sets out with the goal to fail. That's not what I'm suggesting. Failures are simply part of the process of trying new things and taking risks. They are often the stepping-stones in our journey toward success. I would even argue that our greatest failures in life make possible our greatest successes.

The only people who do not fail are the ones who do not try. But not trying is not an acceptable excuse for avoiding failure. In fact, not trying is a condition worse than failure. But, I'm not really talking about failure. At the very core what I'm talking about is *succeeding*. In order to have a positive outlook for trying something new I believe it is important to have permission to fail. If you try to do something new, innovative, or risky, it is very possible that you will fail before you succeed. The main purpose of this book is to inspire Christian entrepreneurs, businesspeople, artists, musicians, students, inventors, and anyone who is interested in discovering the possibilities of a supernatural business life, without the fear of failure.

THE ONLY PEOPLE WHO DO NOT FAIL ARE THE ONES WHO DO NOT TRY.

God looks for people who seek Him and will follow the desires He has placed in their hearts regardless of what the path to achieving those desires looks like. God does not expect you to get it all right as you set out to follow Him.

God knows you may stumble along the way. He is looking for those who are willing to step out and follow the vision He has placed in their hearts.

If you fail along the way, who cares! God will make straight your path and keep you headed in the right direction if you keep your eyes fixed on Jesus.

Prayer

Lord, I choose to hide myself in You and give to You all that I do in my life. Help me to learn from my mistakes and failures so I may come out of them stronger than before. Help me to keep my focus on You and to freely pursue the desires You have placed in my heart, with You leading my way. Amen.

Exercise

✍ Take a moment and write down five times you failed.

✍ What did you learn each time? Who did you meet during the experience? How did you feel immediately after the failure? How do you feel now? How has your perception of the events changed? Write down all that comes to mind.

DAY 22

BOUNCING BACK FROM FAILURE

*This is what the Lord says: "When people fall
down, don't they get up again? When they discover
they're on the wrong road, don't they turn back?"*

Jeremiah 8:4 NLT

It's critically important to understand exactly what to do after failure occurs, because failure certainly will come. Failure happens for everyone. But it is not the end. God still wants to use you in powerful ways! Don't believe me? Let's look at some of the failures of the greatest characters in the Bible.

I saw this poster in my friend's office entitled "Weak Things." It listed some of the greatest men and women in the Bible. But instead of calling out their successes, the poster listed their failures. It went something like this, "Seriously think God can't use you?! Noah was a drunk. Abraham was too old. Jacob was a liar. Moses had a stuttering problem. Gideon was afraid. David had an affair and was a murderer. Elijah was suicidal. Jonah ran from God. Job went bankrupt. Peter denied Christ. The Samaritan woman was divorced. Zacchaeus was too small. Paul was too religious. Lazarus was dead!"

The point is very simply this: not one of God's chosen people is perfect. They all failed at some point. Some had big failures. Some had major character flaws. Despite all their shortcomings, God still used them in mighty ways. And He wants to do the same for you!

In order to be effective in God's Kingdom and to truly build a great business or enterprise in your life, you need to be able to rebound from failure. Here are three key things to do immediately after a failure to help you bounce back quickly and get back on track.

NOT ONE OF GOD'S CHOSEN PEOPLE IS PERFECT. THEY ALL FAILED AT SOME POINT.

First, the moment you enter into a failure, stop, pause, and take inventory of your situation. Ask yourself how you got there. What behaviors or actions led to this point? Who has been impacted besides you? If you arrived at failure pursuing something you presumably believed would lead to success, the absolute first thing you need to do is understand how you got there.

Second, forgive yourself and anyone you may have been hurt by along the way. The first person you may look to blame is yourself. Avoid thinking or saying things like, "I shouldn't have made that decision in the first place." That's not fair to yourself. You made your decision with the knowledge you had at the time. Don't beat yourself up over it. And don't get beaten up by someone else who might blame you for the failure. In order to move past the failure with a clean and pure heart, you need to forgive yourself and others.

Third, reflect and plan for the future. After you have forgiven yourself and others, it's time to clearly think about what went wrong so you can plan your course of action moving forward. I don't believe that anything is truly a failure in the entrepreneurial journey. I only believe there are learning experiences. Oftentimes our greatest failures teach us the most. I know for a fact that I am more equipped and better off for the future having failed at things in the past. Put the knowledge gained through failure into action today.

Prayer

Lord, thank You for Your grace during times of failure. I know that I will get back up when I fall down, as Your Word says so! Help me to forgive myself and others when I go through challenging times, and help me to keep my eyes fixed on Jesus as I pursue the dreams You have put in my heart. Amen.

Exercise

✐ Think of a time you failed that still bothers you when you think about it. Write it down.

✍ Apply these steps to the memory you have of the experience: 1) Accept what happened and ask God to come in and touch the area of your heart that was impacted by this event. 2) Let out your frustration and regret by giving it fully to God. Go for a hike, cry out in the woods, journal out your thoughts—do whatever you need to do to release the emotions from this event. 3) Reflect and ask the Lord to show you what you learned, what you gained, and all the good that came as a result of this event. 4) Move forward with God and leave the regret and frustration behind.

✍ Do these steps any time you experience a failure in life.

BLESSINGS

God's desire is for His people to be blessed. All throughout the Scriptures God reveals keys to accessing the blessings of His Kingdom. These blessings are ours for the taking. We simply need to grab hold of them through faith.

These next four days are devoted to revealing God's blessings.

Taste and see that the Lord is good; blessed is the one who takes refuge in him.

Psalm 34:8 NIV

DAY 23

GOD WANTS YOU TO BE BLESSED

*He who pays attention to the word [of God] will
find good, and blessed (happy, prosperous, to be
admired) is he who trusts [confidently] in the Lord.*

Proverbs 16:20 AMP

*The Lord blessed the latter part of Job's life
more than the former part. He had fourteen
thousand sheep, six thousand camels, a thousand
yoke of oxen and a thousand donkeys.*

Job 42:12 NIV

When studying scripture, a helpful exercise is to look up certain words in the dictionary as you are reading. This provides a new way for understanding the meaning of specific words used throughout the Bible. According to the dictionary, the word *blessed* holds the following meanings: 1) divinely or supremely favored; fortunate; 2) blissfully happy or contented.

The Lord's will for His children is for us to be blessed. It is plainly stated as a promise in His Word. It is important to have revelation of this very simple and straightforward truth: God loves you and desires that you be blessed.

Despite what circumstances or obstacles we may face as we make our way through life, God's word doesn't lie—*blessed is he who trusts in the Lord!*

AS WE NAVIGATE THROUGH THE VARIOUS TWISTS AND TURNS OF LIFE, IF WE PUT OUR TRUST IN THE LORD AND ABIDE IN HIS WORD, WE WILL BE BLESSED.

What happens if you don't feel blessed? What does it mean about God's will for your life if you are currently experiencing a circumstance that doesn't look so blessed? It means absolutely nothing! Take Job for example. He was one of the most blessed people written about in the

Bible. God's Word describes Job as a blameless man of great integrity and one of the richest in the land that he lived. Job is also famously remembered as having endured some of the worst struggles, losses, and challenges that any single person can go through in life. He lost his family and his wealth, and he suffered great physical torment and attacks. Yet trials and losses were merely a temporary period in Job's life. The Lord blessed the latter part of Job's life even greater than the beginning.

No matter what we do in life, it is important to trust in the Lord's desire for us to live a blessed life. This doesn't mean we won't face struggles. This doesn't mean we won't have losses. What it does mean is that, as we navigate through the various twists and turns of life, if we put our trust in the Lord and abide in His Word, we will be blessed.

Understanding this is particularly helpful in starting and running businesses. There will be ups and downs. You might try something new and creative in your business and it might fail. Failing is a part of venturing into something new. There is a saying in Silicon Valley to "fail fast, fail often." One failed attempt does not mean total failure. Your current situation does not dictate your outcome. God will guide your outcome. If you put your trust in the Lord, whatever you do shall prosper. It has to because God's Word says it will.

> *Blessed is the man who walks not in the counsel of the ungodly, nor stands in the path of sinners, nor sits in the seat of the scornful; but his delight is in the law of the Lord* (Psalm 1:1-2).

Prayer

Lord, I ask that You would give me revelation of Your blessings in my life. Show me what it means to delight in the law of the Lord. Help me to trust confidently in You so that You may show me a truly blessed life according to Your promises. Amen.

Exercise

✐ Name three areas of your life that don't currently feel blessed. They could be personal, business, family, financial, or anything else that comes to mind.

_____

_____

_____

✐ How have these things impacted you or made you feel?

_____

_____

_____

_____

✐ Give them over to the Lord and declare God's promise for you to be blessed! Ask God to give you a vision of how He is turning these situations around so that you may be blessed.

DAY 24

BLESSINGS COME TO THOSE WHO FOLLOW THE LORD

So on that day Moses swore to me, "The land on which your feet have walked will be your inheritance and that of your children forever, because you have followed the Lord my God wholeheartedly."

Joshua 14:9 NIV

Joshua and Caleb were two faithful men of God who came out of Egypt with the Israelites through the Red Sea and into the wilderness. They were among those selected to explore the Promised Land and report back to Moses. They saw that the Promised Land indeed flowed with milk and honey and that it was as good as they all had dreamed it would be. There was only one small problem. A very powerful people fortified the land. In order to possess the land, the Israelites had to go and take it. When Joshua and Caleb reported this to the Israelites they were all afraid to go and take the land, even though the Lord was with them. Joshua and Caleb were the only ones with the bravery and faith to go into the Promised Land and possess that which the Lord had promised them.

As a result of their fear, the Israelites would have to stay in the wilderness for 40 years. The Bible says that anyone who was over the age of 20 years old at the time of Joshua and Caleb's report of the Promised Land would ultimately die in the wilderness. Joshua and Caleb were the only two grown adults who left Egypt to have the opportunity to enter the Promised Land.

As the Bible states in Numbers 14:24, the Lord spoke, *"But because my servant Caleb has a different spirit and follows me wholeheartedly, I will bring him into the land he went to, and his descendants will inherit it"* (NIV).

The Bible describes Caleb as a man with a "different spirit" than the other Israelites. He was a man who wholeheartedly followed the Lord. As a result, the Lord recognized his special heart and promised Caleb a great inheritance. That being said, it would take over 45 years for Caleb to receive his inheritance. After crossing over into the Promised Land, 40 years after the Lord promised a great inheritance to him, Caleb declared the Lord's promise before Joshua, and Joshua gave him his allotment in the Promised Land. He was 85 years old at the time he received his inheritance.

> THINGS MAY HAPPEN IN LIFE, AND IN BUSINESS, THAT DELAY US FROM REAPING OUR REWARD. HOWEVER, IF WE REMAIN FOCUSED ON GOD AND FOLLOW HIM WHOLEHEARTEDLY, WE TOO CAN REAP A GREAT BLESSING.

This story is powerful for two very distinct reasons. First, it indicates that God looks upon the heart of a person and rewards those who seek after Him. That is ultimately what God saw in Caleb, which made way for the great blessings he received. Second, God is not one to follow a specific timeline. Things may happen in life, and in business, that delay us from reaping our reward. However, if we remain focused on God and follow Him wholeheartedly, we too can reap a great blessing. It took Caleb 45 years before he received his inheritance. It doesn't always take a long time, but if you find yourself in a situation where you have not yet realized the full blessing of the Lord in your life or business, that doesn't mean it won't come!

Prayer

Lord, I choose to seek You wholeheartedly and to put my worship of You first in my life. Just as Caleb was a man who followed You wholeheartedly, I desire to follow You first and foremost in my life and in all things. Amen.

Exercise

✍ List three things you have been waiting on God for. What are they? How long have you been desiring these blessings in your life? Why do you desire them? Write it all down.

✍ Ask God to reveal hidden keys in your life that may open the door for receiving these blessings. Write down what God shows you.

_____

_____

_____

_____

_____

✍ Recommit your heart to wholeheartedly follow God just like Caleb. Write out your own declaration and commitment to follow God in your business pursuits.

_____

_____

_____

_____

_____

DAY 25

YOUR LIFE IS A BLESSING TO OTHERS

The Lord was with Joseph, so he succeeded in everything he did as he served in the home of his Egyptian master. Potiphar noticed this and realized that the Lord was with Joseph, giving him success in everything he did. This pleased Potiphar, so he soon made Joseph his personal attendant. He put him in charge of his entire household and everything he owned.

Genesis 39:2-4 NLT

The well-known story of Joseph's life is one of the many great examples of how God uses all circumstances to bless His people. Not only does God desire to bless His people, He desires to use His people to be a blessing to others. Joseph was the youngest of eleven sons, and the Bible describes how Joseph's father loved him more than all of his other sons because he had been born to him in his old age. Because he was highly favored by their father, Joseph's brothers were very jealous of this and hated him as a result. Joseph was not only highly favored by his father, but he was also very gifted spiritually by God and had many prophetic dreams. Ultimately, Joseph's brothers, consumed by their jealousy of Joseph, faked Joseph's death and sold their brother into slavery. Once in slavery, Joseph was transported and sold in Egypt to Potiphar, one of Pharaoh's high officials.

> WHEN WE STAY CLOSE TO THE LORD DESPITE OUR SITUATION, **WE HAVE ACCESS TO THE LORD'S BLESSINGS.**

Despite Joseph's situation and having been betrayed by his own family, what happened next is truly remarkable. The Lord was with Joseph and he prospered when he was in the house of his Egyptian master. Joseph found favor in the eyes of his master and Potiphar even put him in charge of his entire household, entrusting to Joseph the care of everything he owned. That is quite a responsibility and authority for a slave!

From the time he put him in charge of his household and of all that he owned, the Lord blessed the household of the Egyptian because of Joseph. The blessing of the Lord was on everything Potiphar had, both in the house and in the field. So Potiphar left everything he had in Joseph's care; with Joseph in charge, he did not concern himself with anything except the food he ate (Genesis 39:5-6 NIV).

It's hard to imagine that someone can flourish personally, spiritually, and financially when in slavery. But that's exactly what happened with Joseph. God uses every situation in our lives to bring about blessings for us, as well as to use us to bless others. When we stay close to the Lord despite our situation, we have access to the Lord's blessings.

Before I took the leap as an entrepreneur myself, I often felt confined, limited, and out of place. Working a nine-to-five corporate job wasn't my unique purpose in life. God called me to create, build things, and start companies of my own. When I was working for other people it just never felt right. During my career, when working at other people's companies I always prayed for the grace and strength to do my job well. I would often pray throughout the office and invite the Holy Spirit into the work environment. As a result, I was always blessed in my career work when employed by other people. The Lord used me to be a blessing to others in the workplace and He used my career journey to open up the door to life as an entrepreneur.

Prayer

Lord, I ask that You would give me revelation of how You want to use me to bless others. Be with me in the work I do. Give me favor with Your people and open up doors for Your supernatural blessings in my life. Amen.

Exercise

✍ List three people you have been a blessing to in your business life. How has God used you to bless them? What has been the fruit?

_____

_____

_____

_____

✍ Ask God to highlight three new people He wants you to be a blessing to. How are you connected? What practical steps can you take today to start being a blessing to them? Write down what God shows you.

_____

_____

_____

_____

DAY 26

PRAISE USHERS IN BLESSINGS

Enter his gates with thanksgiving and his courts with praise; give thanks to him and praise his name.

Psalm 100:4 NIV

But You are holy, enthroned in the praises of Israel.

Psalm 22:3

By praising God we make room for the blessings of heaven to flow in our lives. Praising the Lord gets the focus off of ourselves and puts the focus directly on God, which is our highest command as Christians. We see this very clearly from Jesus' own words in Matthew 22:37-38: *"'Love the Lord your God with every passion of your heart, with all the energy of your being, and with every thought that is within you.' This is the great and supreme commandment"* (TPT).

WHEN WE POSITION OUR HEARTS IN SUCH A WAY WE ARE NOT ONLY BEING OBEDIENT TO THE SUPREME COMMANDMENT, **WE ARE ENTERING INTO A PLACE WHERE THE BLESSINGS OF HEAVEN CAN FLOW FREELY INTO OUR LIVES.**

Not only are we commanded to praise the Lord and give Him all of our affection, it is something that opens up great blessings in our lives. Now, don't set out to praise God with the very intention of receiving blessings. Your heart must be postured in such a way that your entire being is surrendered and devoted to pursuing and praising the Lord. When we position our hearts in such a way we are not only being obedient to the supreme commandment, we are entering into a place where the blessings of heaven can flow freely into our lives.

Psalm 22:3 declares that God is enthroned in the praises of Israel. This is often interpreted as "God inhabits the praises of His people." When we praise God and we give our full heart in worship, as we pursue Him, He comes to be present with us. An analogy I've often used to describe the relationship between praise and the presence of God is through the illustration of an earthly father. If children are playing about the house and run into their father's office and proclaim something as simple as "Daddy, I love you," it delights the father's heart. My father in particular would stop what he was doing to spend time with me and my siblings if we simply ran up to him, jumped on his lap, and expressed our love to him. These unplanned moments often made for some of our fondest memories with our dad growing up.

Let's think about that scenario from the perspective of praising and worshiping God. If we give God our hearts in worship, He comes to listen to His children give Him praise! This is manifested in the presence of the Holy Spirit who inhabits our praises. It is the presence of God that makes way for blessings, miracles, and supernatural manifestations of His glory here on earth as it is in heaven.

IF WE CREATE A CULTURE OF PRAISE AND WORSHIP THROUGHOUT OUR BUSINESSES, WE CAN CREATE AN ATMOSPHERE FOR GOD TO INHABIT OUR BUSINESS.

Now, let's think about what praise can do for our businesses. It can do the same thing! If we create a culture of praise and worship throughout our businesses, we can create an atmosphere for God to inhabit our business. Whether you are facing an obstacle, going in for a big investor pitch, or simply desiring to manage your team with excellence, a culture of praise and worship, flowing from the office of the business owner, will permeate every aspect of your business and make way for the supernatural blessings of heaven to flow.

Prayer

Abba Father, I give You all my praises. I put my whole heart into praising You, for You are so good. I invite You to inhabit my life and work as I submit my heart and will fully to Yours. Create in me a culture of praise and worship in all that I do and let it be obvious to everyone around me. Amen.

Exercise

✎ Take some time to praise and worship God for the next five to ten minutes.

✎ Then think of three areas of your life that you are seeking breakthrough. Write them down and lay them in the middle of the room. Then go back into praising and worshiping God specifically over these things in your life. Do this as a daily practice for the next few weeks and take notice of what changes.

✎ Next, start doing this as a daily practice over your business. Watch the blessings and breakthrough of God come into your business as you give Him all your praise and worship. Write down how doing this positively impacts your business over time.

ACTION

We can talk about how God wants to bless us, but until we put action behind our words we won't see any fruit from it. God blesses those who work hard and sow into their vision and dreams with action.

These next four days are devoted to activating you to step out and take action toward your goals and vision for life.

For the kingdom of God is not a matter of talk but of power.

1 Corinthians 4:20 NIV

DAY 27

HARD WORK PAYS OFF

*Hard work means prosperity; only
a fool idles away his time.*

Proverbs 12:11 TLB

The dictionary is the only place that
success comes before work. Work is
the key to success, and hard work can
help you accomplish anything.

—Vince Lombardi

Unless you are the beneficiary of a big inheritance you will have to work for your success. That's just the way it is. However, that's also a central part of God's plan. Humans were created to be workers. In Genesis 2:15 the Bible says that after God created man and woman the Lord God took the man and put him in the Garden of Eden to work it and take care of it. Humans weren't created to just exist in the world. We were created to work in the world that God created. We have a complex brain that is capable of intelligence, reasoning, and creativity. We have hands that we can use to build and create the things thought up by our minds. God created the earth, and all that is in it, and He created humans to work and labor on earth to maintain it and to produce new things.

IF YOU DESIRE TO BE AN ENTREPRENEUR, IT IS GOING TO BE HARD WORK.

The imagery of the Garden of Eden and God's command for humans to work is crystal clear. It is even clearer for folks who have actually tried gardening. It's especially clear for folks who have tried gardening in Texas during the summer! The simple truth about gardening is that if you do not tend to your garden it will not be fruitful and it will likely die. Gardens need watering. Plants require pruning. Gardens need to be protected from predators such as bugs and other animals that will destroy your plants. It takes a lot of hard work to maintain a healthy garden. God knows that. His instructions to Adam and Eve in the Garden of Eden included a full understanding that it would be hard work. Thankfully, that hard work would not be futile—quite the opposite! God's design for humanity is for us to work hard and to prosper in the fruits of our labor.

God's Word is very specific. If we work hard, we will prosper (see Prov. 12:11). If you desire to be an entrepreneur, it is going to be hard work. That's the truth. The hard work is an investment we make in ourselves. By definition, an investment is something that brings a reward. If you invest money by purchasing stock, and the price of the stock goes up, the reward is an appreciation in value, which is realized through cash income. Similar to making an investment in stock to gain a cash reward, the principle of hard work is the same in God's Kingdom. If you work hard, you will reap a reward. This reward may take the form of money, favor, relationships, opportunities, or something else. Whatever form the reward takes, the outcome is that you will be blessed. God makes this very clear all throughout Scripture.

Lazy people want much but get little, but those who work hard will prosper (Proverbs 13:4 NLT).

Prayer

Father God, I thank You that my hard work will result in blessings. Your Word tells me so. Help me to understand the value of my hard work and that my time spent working hard is an investment in my life. Like any investment, I declare that I shall reap a reward for my hard work. Thank You, Jesus! Amen.

Exercise

✍ Write down three times you built something. It could be anything—a craft, school project, business, website— you name it.

✍ What was it like working on these things? Was it difficult or challenging? How did you feel during the process?

✍ What did it feel like to complete these things? What was the fruit of your hard work?

DAY 28

YOU ARE WORKING FOR THE LORD

Work willingly at whatever you do, as though you were working for the Lord rather than for people. Remember that the Lord will give you an inheritance as your reward, and that the Master you are serving is Christ.

Colossians 3:23-24 NLT

God created us to be creators. When we work hard and put our hands to something, we are doing what God created us to do. In all that we do, we are actually doing it for God. God delights in seeing His creation work hard. This is the most important thing we need to remember as Christian entrepreneurs. According to Scripture, it is God who gives us the ability to generate wealth, *"But remember the Lord your God, for it is he who gives you the ability to produce wealth, and so confirms his covenant, which he swore to your ancestors, as it is today"* (Deut. 8:18 NIV).

As entrepreneurs, we don't technically have a boss, as we are working for ourselves. Scripture exhorts us to work as though we are working for the Lord. What does that actually mean? I take it to mean that we are to work as though God is our boss, as though every action we take and decision we make is made in an effort to glorify God. Sure, we may not have a physical boss in the natural, but we need to work as though the Lord is our boss. To do so means we conduct ourselves with integrity and godly character in all that we do.

As an entrepreneur you will face obstacles, challenges, and uphill climbs all the time. When working at a larger company you have the privilege of going to the HR department when you have an issue or asking your supervisor for help. As an entrepreneur, you are the HR department and your own supervisor. There isn't a department to go to for help. You have to figure out what to do. This would be an incredibly nerve-wracking environment to live in if it weren't for God. As a Christian entrepreneur, God is your very present help! As the Psalmist wrote in Psalm 46:1-2, *"God is a safe place to hide, ready to help when we need him. We stand fearless at the cliff-edge of doom, courageous in sea storm and earthquake"* (MSG).

As Christians in business, we play by a different playbook than the secular business world. We have the God of heaven and earth on our side! But we still face the same challenges, if not more than the rest of the world. Peter writes, *"Be sober, be vigilant; because your adversary the devil walks about like a roaring lion, seeking whom he may devour. Resist him, steadfast in the faith, knowing that the same sufferings are experienced by your brotherhood in the world"* (1 Pet. 5:8-9).

AS CHRISTIANS IN BUSINESS, WE PLAY BY A DIFFERENT PLAYBOOK THAN THE SECULAR BUSINESS WORLD. WE HAVE THE GOD OF HEAVEN AND EARTH ON OUR SIDE!

Yes, we will face challenges as entrepreneurs, both physical and spiritual. However, through our faith in God we can successfully resist the attacks of the enemy and overcome the physical challenges that we will face in business. To do this, it is critically important to always remember that we are working for the Lord, not ourselves. Every action we take is for the Lord.

Prayer

*Father God, help me to understand that You
are my actual boss. I submit my work to You,
because You are the Lord of my life. I choose to
trust that, with You in charge of my work, I will
be blessed and reap a mighty inheritance. Amen.*

Exercise

✍ Think of two or three times your boss, or someone senior to you, asked you to do something you didn't really feel like doing but was a part of your job.

✍ How did these moments make you feel? How did you respond? Did you honor the authority figure in your life joyfully or begrudgingly?

✍ Now think about if Jesus Himself had asked you to do something. How would you respond differently if it were Jesus asking you to do these things?

DAY 29

ACCESSING THE CREATIVE NATURE OF GOD

And if the Spirit of him who raised Jesus from the dead is living in you, he who raised Christ from the dead will also give life to your mortal bodies because of his Spirit who lives in you.

Romans 8:11 NIV

The moment we accept Jesus Christ as our Lord and Savior an instantaneous miracle takes place. We become filled with the Holy Spirit. Our bodies become the temple that God makes His home.

The first time this powerful truth became a personal revelation to me I nearly fell out of my chair. I'm sure we've all read this verse or have heard it in church at one point or another. When the Word goes from Scripture on a page to personal revelation, that's when transformation can take place.

"The Spirit of him who raised Jesus from the dead is living in you." Consider the power of that statement for a moment. That spirit is the Spirit of God, the same spirit that hovered over the mist and created earth and all of creation.

> *In the beginning God created the heavens and the earth. The earth was without form, and void; and darkness was on the face of the deep. And the Spirit of God was hovering over the face of the waters* (Genesis 1:1-2).

As Christians, we possess the creative nature of God because God's Spirit dwells within us. We have the power and the authority on earth to create new things, inventions, businesses, technology, and more. Ever since the beginning of life, God has been looking to man to be His co-creator. God created every living creature then brought them to Adam to name them.

> *Out of the ground the Lord God formed every beast of the field and every bird of the air, and brought them to Adam to see what he would call them. And whatever Adam called each living creature, that was its name* (Genesis 2:19).

WITH CHRIST DWELLING IN US GOD HAS GIVEN US MORE THAN THE AUTHORITY TO NAME. HE HAS GIVEN US THE POWER TO CREATE.

God created every living thing, then gave Adam the authority to name them. That's like Bill Gates creating an operating system then bringing it to his son and asking him to name it. With Christ dwelling in us God has given us more than the authority to name. He has given us the power to create. It's time for Christians to step up to the plate and grab hold of the power that is already within us.

The next great technology innovation, the cure to cancer, the electric car that can travel 10,000 miles on a single charge, the next best ice cream flavor—these are all things that Christians have the power to create. The source of the creativity of the entire universe dwells inside of every believer. We need only to seek God in prayer and He will show us how to create new things that can change the world.

Prayer

Lord, I come to You, the Creator of all things, and I ask for fresh revelation of my creative abilities. Show me what it truly means to have Your Spirit dwelling inside of me. Show me how to live a supernatural business life and bring the creative power and authority that You have given me into my business. Amen.

Exercise

✍ Spend some time in prayer and ask God to give you five new business ideas. They could be anything from technology, inventions, a small business, a store, or anything that comes to mind. Nothing is off-limits.

✍ Now pick one and create a one-page business plan for it.

✍ What's the problem you are trying to solve?

✍ What's your solution to this problem?

_____

_____

_____

_____

✍ What is your unique value proposition?

_____

_____

_____

_____

✍ Who are your target customers?

_____

_____

_____

_____

🖎 How will the business make money?

_____

_____

_____

_____

🖎 What will the costs be?

_____

_____

_____

_____

🖎 What will the revenue streams be?

_____

_____

_____

_____

🖎 Next, pitch it to a family member or friend this week. Simply ask them, "Hey, would you mind if I shared my business idea with you?" Be bold and pitch it! Ask them for their feedback and don't be concerned if they don't like it!

DAY 30

LIFE IS SHORT. MAKE IT COUNT!

Look here, you who say, "Today or tomorrow we are going to a certain town and will stay there a year. We will do business there and make a profit." How do you know what your life will be like tomorrow? Your life is like the morning fog—it's here a little while, then it's gone.

James 4:13-14 NLT

What if I told you your time on earth is limited? What if I told you that you are going to die? I'm not trying to provoke you to fear and I am definitely not prophesying your early death! I'm illustrating a simple fact. The time we have in life is limited and finite. In James 4:14, in the English Standard Version, the Bible describes the ephemerality of life in this way, "You are a mist that appears for a little time and then vanishes." This scripture is not intended to cause fear, but it illustrates a simple set of facts: 1) our time is limited; 2) we must use our time wisely in order to have the most impact.

Steve Jobs was once quoted as saying, "When you grow up you tend to get told that the world is the way it is and your life is just to live your life inside the world. Try not to bash into the walls too much. Try to have a nice family life, have fun, save a little money. That's a very limited life. Life can be much broader once you discover one simple fact: everything around you that you call life was made up by people that were no smarter than you. And you can change it, you can influence it. Once you learn that, you'll never be the same again."

Steve Jobs' words are powerful in the simple truth they reveal. The people who are out there having success are no better or smarter than you are. The only difference between people who succeed and those who do not is that the people who succeed put action behind their words. They are taking risks, trying new things, and testing their ideas on a daily basis. They risk failure daily, and that's why they succeed. But these people are no smarter than you! You can do it to. Anyone can do it. You can have a big impact with the life God has given you. It all starts with stepping out, taking a risk, and going for it. Without trying, without taking action, it is impossible to achieve anything.

Michael Jordan famously said, "I've missed more than 9,000 shots in my career. I've lost almost 300 games. Twenty-six times I've been trusted to take the game winning shot and missed. I've failed over and over and over again in my life. And that is why I succeed." Another often unknown fact about Michael Jordan is that he was originally cut from the varsity basketball team in high school. As he tells the story, he ran home after not making the varsity team roster, locked himself in his room, and cried. It was a crushing blow to his dream of playing basketball, but it wasn't the end of his story. What he did after this failure is what defined his life and led him to become the greatest basketball player who ever lived. He turned being cut from the varsity team into motivation, training harder, and practicing more than anyone else. He then made the varsity team the following season and the rest is history.

The only difference between winning and losing is the hard work and consistent effort that winners put into achieving their dreams. Life is short. Put in the hard work and it will pay off. Get started today!

THE ONLY DIFFERENCE BETWEEN WINNING AND LOSING IS THE HARD WORK AND CONSISTENT EFFORT THAT WINNERS PUT INTO ACHIEVING THEIR DREAMS.

Prayer

Father God, I thank You for all the opportunities You have given me in my life. Cultivate in me a work ethic of excellence, perseverance, and grit. Give me the courage, resolve, and strength to pursue new things, take risks, and keep going when things get tough. Amen.

Exercise

✍ For the final day's exercise think back on the last 30 days.

✍ What have you learned about yourself during this time?

_____

_____

_____

_____

_____

✍ What has God imparted to you as you explored Him and got to know yourself better?

_____

_____

_____

_____

_____

✍ What do you plan to do with what you've gained?

_____

_____

_____

_____

_____

✍ What will you build from here?

_____

_____

_____

_____

_____

Notes

ABOUT MATT BELL

Matthew Bell is a prophetic businessman and serial entrepreneur. He is impassioned by the desire to see God's people unlock their supernatural gifts for application in the realm of business and entrepreneurship. His greatest hope is to see the church rise up and access supernatural strategies from heaven to transform culture through innovative business and technology.

.

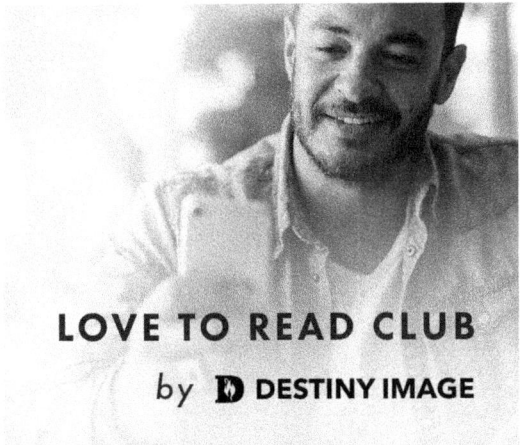

www.ingramcontent.com/pod-product-compliance
Lightning Source LLC
Chambersburg PA
CBHW071407160426